Powered by the Spirit:
Growing in Kindness and Forgiveness

Middle School

Self-Published by
Alisa L. Grace
Sanford, FL 32771

ISBN: 978-1-966129-70-7

First Edition

Printed in the United States of America

Library of Congress Cataloging-in-Publication Data
Grace, Alisa L.
Title of the Book: Powered by the Spirit: Middle School Growing in Kindness and Forgiveness
Library of Congress Control Number: 2025903446

Disclaimer: The views expressed in this book are those of the author and do not necessarily reflect any organizations or individuals mentioned.

Acknowledgments: The author wishes to thank God, Her Husband (Linion), Victory Temple of God, Florida SPECS, Unity Youth Association, All About Serving You, Angels-ANJ Events, NordeVest, and Love & Create Life for their support and contributions.

Dedication:

This book is dedicated to all the young
hearts seeking to understand the power of the Holy Spirit in
their lives, especially as they navigate the exciting and sometimes
challenging world of friendships.

A Letter to Parents

Dear Parents,

This book is designed to be a valuable tool in introducing your middle school child to the concept of the Holy Spirit and its role in their daily lives. As children enter their pre-teen years, they encounter increasingly complex social and emotional situations, especially within their friendships. "Powered by the Spirit" aims to guide them through these challenges, emphasizing the importance of kindness, forgiveness, and relying on the Holy Spirit for wisdom and peace.

This book provides a relatable narrative that explores common friendship struggles, such as misunderstandings, hurt feelings, and the process of reconciliation. Through the characters' experiences, children will learn how to:

- Identify the Holy Spirit's presence in their lives.
- Seek guidance from the Holy Spirit in handling difficult emotions and situations.
- Practice kindness and forgiveness, even when it's challenging.
- Communicate effectively and resolve conflicts peacefully.

We encourage you to read this book alongside your child, engaging in discussions about the themes presented and helping them apply these principles to their own lives. By fostering an understanding of the Holy Spirit's empowering presence, we can equip our children to navigate their relationships with grace, empathy, and resilience.

A Letter to the Middle School Student

Hey there, awesome middle schooler!

Ever felt lost or confused when dealing with a tough situation with a friend? Like, you don't know what to say or do? This book is here to help! It's like a toolbox filled with tips and tricks to help you handle those tricky friendship moments.

Inside, you'll meet Ahlani, Nia, and Lenny – they're just like you, figuring out friendships, dealing with hurt feelings, and learning how to forgive. They'll show you that there's an amazing power inside you – the Holy Spirit – that can guide you through anything.

This book is your guide to understanding how the Holy Spirit can help you:

- Stay calm when you're angry or upset.
- Find the words to talk about your feelings.
- Forgive others, even when it's super hard.
- Build stronger and kinder friendships.

Get ready to unlock the power within and discover how to make your friendships even more amazing!

Contents

Introduction

Have you ever felt a nudge to do something kind, even when you didn't feel like it? Or maybe you've felt a sense of peace wash over you during a stressful situation. That, my friend, could be the Holy Spirit at work!

The Holy Spirit is like a secret superpower that God gives us. It's a constant companion, a guide, and a source of strength who's always there to help us. But sometimes, we get so busy or distracted that we forget to listen to its gentle whispers.

That's where this book comes in! "Powered by the Spirit: Growing in Kindness and Forgiveness" is your guide to discovering how the Holy Spirit can help you navigate the ups and downs of friendships.

Inside these pages, Ahlani, Nia, and Lenny are three friends learning to rely on the Holy Spirit as they face challenges and misunderstandings. You'll see how the Holy Spirit helps them:

> **Stay calm when they're angry or upset:** Have you ever felt like exploding when someone hurts your feelings? The Holy Spirit can help you find your cool and respond in a way that brings peace, not more drama.

> **Find the words to talk about their feelings:** Sometimes, explaining what's going on inside is hard. The Holy Spirit can help you find the right words to express yourself clearly and honestly.

Forgive others, even when it's super hard: Forgiveness can be challenging, especially when someone has really hurt you. But the Holy Spirit can strengthen you to release anger and resentment.

Build stronger and kinder friendships: The Holy Spirit can help you be a better friend by showing you how to be kind, compassionate, and understanding.

This book is filled with exciting stories, fun activities, and thought-provoking questions that will help you discover the incredible power of the Holy Spirit in your own life. Get ready to unlock your inner superpower and learn to grow in kindness and forgiveness!

Chapter 1:
The Conflict Among Friends

Purpose:

To introduce the characters and set the stage for a relatable conflict between friends, highlighting the complex emotions that arise during disagreements.

Story: Ahlani and Nia, best friends since kindergarten, were inseparable. They giggled over silly jokes, shared secrets in hushed whispers, and dreamed of exciting futures together. With his infectious laugh and knack for adventure, Lenny was a welcome addition to their close-knit circle. But lately, a shadow had fallen over their friendship.

It all started during a history class group project. They were creating a presentation about ancient Egypt, and Lenny caught up in his enthusiasm, blurted out, "Nia, you should be the pharaoh! You'd look great in that gold headdress, with all that... you know... hair!" He gestured vaguely towards Nia's thick, curly Afro.

A wave of heat crept up Nia's neck. Lenny's comment, though likely meant to be lighthearted, stung. It wasn't the first time someone had commented on her hair, and it always left her feeling singled out and uncomfortable. A forced smile plastered on her face as she mumbled, "Yeah, funny, Lenny," but hurt and anger simmered inside.

Later that day, Nia confided in Ahlani, her voice thick with emotion. "He just doesn't get it," she explained, tears welling in her eyes. "It's not a joke, Ahlani. It makes me feel like he doesn't respect me." Ahlani listened, her brow furrowed with concern. She knew these weren't the trivial spats they used to have over whose turn it was to pick the game. This was different, deeper. This was about respect, identity, and the complexities of navigating friendships as they grew older.

Transformative Question: Have you ever felt misunderstood or hurt by a friend's words or actions? How did it make you feel?

_____

_____

_____

_____

_____

_____

_____

_____

_____

_____

_____

_____

_____

_____

_____

_____

_____

_____

_____

_____

_____

10-Minute Activity: Consider when a friend's words hurt your feelings. How did it make you feel? Write down those feelings in a journal or on a piece of paper. Try to describe the situation and why their words were hurtful.

Chapter 2:
The Guidance
of the Holy Spirit

Purpose:

To introduce the concept of the Holy Spirit as a source of comfort, guidance, and wisdom in challenging situations.

Story: Ahlani, always the thoughtful one, pondered Nia's situation. Just the day before, her Sunday school teacher had spoken about the Holy Spirit – a constant companion, a source of strength and guidance for believers. "The Holy Spirit," her teacher had explained, "is like a gentle whisper in your heart, leading you towards love, kindness, and peace, even when things are hard."

Ahlani shared this with Nia, explaining how the Holy Spirit could help them navigate this difficult situation. "It's about not letting anger take over," she said earnestly. "It's about asking the Holy Spirit to help us see things clearly and find a way to make things right."

Nia, still raw with hurt, was hesitant. But she trusted Ahlani, and the idea of a guiding presence offering comfort and wisdom appealed to her. Together, they bowed their heads and prayed. "Holy Spirit," Ahlani whispered, "please help us. Show us how to handle this situation with kindness and understanding. Help us find peace."

As they finished praying, a sense of calm settled over Ahlani. Nia, too, felt a shift within her. The tight knot of anger in her chest loosened slightly. Maybe Ahlani was right. Maybe there was a way to move forward without staying stuck in this hurt.

Transformative Question: When you're facing a difficult situation, how can you invite the Holy Spirit to guide you?

_____

_____

_____

_____

_____

_____

_____

_____

_____

_____

_____

_____

_____

_____

_____

_____

_____

10-Minute Activity: Find a quiet place where you can be alone. Close your eyes and take slow, deep breaths. Imagine a warm, peaceful feeling inside you. That's the Holy Spirit! Talk to the Holy Spirit silently about anything that's on your mind. You can ask for help, guidance, or simply share your thoughts and feelings.

Chapter 3:
Taking the First Step

Purpose:

To emphasize the importance of communication and taking the initiative to address conflict rather than avoiding it.

Story: Meanwhile, Lenny was oblivious to the turmoil he had caused. He noticed Nia's distance, the way she avoided his eyes in the hallway, and the forced smiles that didn't quite reach her eyes. Confusion gnawed at him. Had he done something wrong?

Ahlani, sensing the growing rift between her friends, knew it was time for action. "Nia," she said gently, "holding onto this anger won't help. You need to talk to Lenny. Explain how you feel."

Nia's heart pounded. Confrontation wasn't her style. But the quiet voice of the Holy Spirit echoed in her mind, urging her to be brave, to choose kindness and communication over silence and resentment. She took a deep breath, her resolve solidifying. It was time to take the first step.

Transformative Question: Why is it important to communicate openly and honestly with your friends, even when it's difficult?

_____

_____

_____

_____

_____

_____

_____

_____

_____

_____

_____

_____

_____

_____

_____

_____

_____

_____

_____

_____

10-Minute Activity: Think about a time you had a disagreement with a friend. What could you have done differently? Write a short letter to that friend (you don't have to send it!) explaining how you felt.

Chapter 4:
Confronting the Issue

Purpose:

To demonstrate how honest and open communication, guided by the Holy Spirit, can lead to understanding and resolution.

Story: After school, Nia, with Ahlani by her side for moral support, approached Lenny. Her palms were sweaty, and her voice trembled slightly as she began to speak. "Lenny," she said, "I need to talk to you about something. The comment you made about my hair during the project... it hurt my feelings."

Lenny's eyes widened in surprise. "Nia, I'm so sorry! I never meant to hurt you. I was just trying to be funny." He looked genuinely remorseful.

Nia continued, "I know you probably didn't mean it that way, but it made me feel uncomfortable. It's not just about my hair, Lenny. It's about respecting me."

Lenny nodded earnestly. "You're right, Nia. I messed up. I should have thought before I spoke. Can you forgive me?"

In that moment, Nia felt a wave of release. Forgiveness, she realized, wasn't about pretending nothing had happened. It was about choosing to let go of anger and resentment, about extending grace and understanding, just as the Holy Spirit had guided her to do.

Transformative Question: How does forgiveness feel? Why is it important to forgive others, even when they've hurt you?

10-Minute Activity: Role-play with a friend or family member. One person pretends to be upset about something, and the other person tries to understand and apologize. Take turns playing each role.

Chapter 5:
Restoring the Friendship

Purpose:

To illustrate the healing power of forgiveness and reconciliation in restoring and strengthening friendships.

Story: A weight lifted from Nia's shoulders. Lenny, visibly relieved, grinned. "So, we're good?" he asked, hope shining in his eyes.

Nia smiled back, a genuine smile this time. "We're good," she confirmed.

Ahlani beamed at her friends. "See?" she said. "Talking things out really does help."

The three friends walked home together, their laughter echoing through the streets. Their friendship, tested by misunderstanding and hurt, emerged stronger and deeper. They had learned a valuable lesson about the power of communication, forgiveness, and the guiding presence of the Holy Spirit.

As they reached Nia's house, she turned to her friends, a newfound sense of gratitude washing over her. "Thanks, you guys," she said sincerely. "Thanks for helping me through this. I was so stuck in being angry, I didn't know what to do."

"That's what friends are for," Ahlani replied, giving Nia a warm hug.

Lenny chimed in, "Yeah, and I'm really sorry again for what I said. I'll be more careful with my words from now on."

Nia squeezed his arm. "I know you will," she said, and they all shared a comfortable silence, their bond renewed and strengthened by their shared experience.

Transformative Question: How does it feel to forgive someone or to be forgiven? How can forgiveness change a friendship?

_____

_____

_____

_____

_____

_____

_____

_____

_____

_____

_____

_____

_____

_____

_____

_____

_____

_____

_____

_____

_____

10-Minute Activity: Draw a picture of you and your friends having fun together. Write down some things you can do to be a kinder and more forgiving friend.

Conclusion:
Growing Together
in Kindness and Forgiveness

Purpose:

To reinforce the key themes of the book and encourage readers to continue relying on the Holy Spirit in their relationships.

Story: Ahlani reflected on the past few days. She realized the Holy Spirit wasn't just present in church on Sundays. It was a constant companion, guiding her choices and prompting her to be kind, patient, and forgiving. She knew that with the Holy Spirit's help, she could navigate the ups and downs of friendships with grace and understanding.

She thought about how the Holy Spirit helped her be a better friend to Nia and Lenny. It gave her the courage to encourage Nia to talk to Lenny and helped Nia find the words to express her feelings. Ahlani knew that even though friendships could be challenging sometimes, the Holy Spirit would always guide her.

Ahlani smiled to herself. She was excited to see what adventures lay ahead with her friends, knowing they could face any challenge with the power of the Holy Spirit.

Key takeaway: The Holy Spirit is always with you, ready to help you grow in kindness and forgiveness. By listening to its gentle guidance, you can build strong, lasting friendships filled with love and understanding.

Encouraging Participation

Dear Friend,

Are you ready to embark on an incredible spiritual growth and discovery journey? I invite you to join me in the **20-Day Challenge: Intentionally Listening to the Spirit.**

This challenge is designed to help you deepen your relationship with the Holy Spirit and become more attuned to its guidance in your daily life. Over the next 20 days, we'll explore different ways to quiet our minds, open our hearts, and listen to the gentle whispers of the Spirit.

Why is this challenge so significant? The Holy Spirit is our constant companion, our source of comfort, wisdom, and strength. When we learn to listen to the Spirit intentionally, we open ourselves to a life of greater peace, joy, and purpose.

Each day, you'll receive a challenge, a supporting scripture, and a call to action to guide your practice. These simple steps will help you cultivate a deeper connection with the Spirit and experience its transformative power.

This challenge can be a powerful catalyst for spiritual growth. Are you ready to take the leap and discover how the Holy Spirit can work in your life?

Join me on this journey!
With blessings,
Alisa L. Grace

20-Day Challenge:
Intentionally Listening to the Spirit

This challenge is designed to help you deepen your relationship with the Holy Spirit and become more attuned to its guidance in your daily life. Each day, you'll focus on a specific aspect of listening to the Spirit, with a challenge, a supporting scripture, and a call to action to guide your practice.

Day 1: Quiet Your Mind

Challenge: Spend 10 minutes in silence, focusing on your breath and stilling your thoughts.

Scripture: "Be still, and know that I am God." - Psalm 46:10

Call to Action: Reflect on any thoughts or feelings that arise during your quiet time. Do you sense the Holy Spirit speaking to you?

Day 2: Read and Reflect

Challenge: Read a passage from the Bible (e.g., John 14:15-17, Romans 8:26-27) and reflect on what it teaches you about the Holy Spirit.

Scripture: "When the Spirit of truth comes, he will guide you into all the truth." - John 16:13

Call to Action: Write down any insights or questions that come to mind as you read and reflect.

_____

_____

_____

_____

_____

_____

_____

_____

_____

_____

_____

_____

_____

_____

_____

_____

_____

Day 3: Pray for Guidance

Challenge: Begin your day with a prayer asking the Holy Spirit to guide your thoughts, words, and actions.

Scripture: "If you then, though you are evil, know how to give good gifts to your children, how much more will your Father in heaven give the Holy Spirit to those who ask him!" - Luke 11:13

Call to Action: Throughout the day, pause to remember your prayer and be open to the Spirit's leading.

_____

_____

_____

_____

_____

_____

_____

_____

_____

_____

_____

_____

_____

_____

_____

_____

Day 4: Practice Gratitude

Challenge: Take time to express gratitude for the ways the Holy Spirit has worked in your life.

Scripture: "But the fruit of the Spirit is love, joy, peace, forbearance, kindness, goodness, faithfulness, gentleness and self-control." - Galatians 5:22-23

Call to Action: Write a thank-you note to God, expressing your gratitude for the Spirit's presence.

Day 5: Be Present

Challenge: Engage fully in your activities today, noticing the details and being present in each moment.

Scripture: "I have set the Lord always before me. Because he is at my right hand, I will not be shaken." - Psalm 16:8

Call to Action: At the end of the day, reflect on how being present allowed you to be more aware of the Spirit's presence.

_____

_____

_____

_____

_____

_____

_____

_____

_____

_____

_____

_____

_____

_____

_____

_____

_____

Day 6: Listen to Others

Challenge: Practice active listening in your conversations, seeking to truly understand others' perspectives.

Scripture: "My dear brothers and sisters, take note of this: Everyone should be quick to listen, slow to speak and slow to become angry." - James 1:19

Call to Action: Consider how listening to others can help you hear the Spirit's voice more clearly.

_____

_____

_____

_____

_____

_____

_____

_____

_____

_____

_____

_____

_____

_____

_____

Day 7: Observe Your Thoughts

Challenge: Pay attention to your thoughts throughout the day. Are they aligned with the fruit of the Spirit?

Scripture: "Finally, brothers and sisters, whatever is true, whatever is noble, whatever is right, whatever is pure, whatever is lovely, whatever is admirable—if anything is excellent or praiseworthy—think about such things." - Philippians 4:8

Call to Action: When you notice negative or unhelpful thoughts, ask the Holy Spirit to help you reframe them.

_____

_____

_____

_____

_____

_____

_____

_____

_____

_____

_____

_____

_____

_____

_____

Day 8: Embrace Solitude

Challenge: Spend some time alone today, even if it's just for a few minutes.

Scripture: "But Jesus often withdrew to lonely places and prayed." - Luke 5:16

Call to Action: Use this time to connect with God and listen for the Spirit's whispers.

_____

_____

_____

_____

_____

_____

_____

_____

_____

_____

_____

_____

_____

_____

_____

_____

_____

_____

Day 9: Serve Others

Challenge: Do something kind for someone else today, without expecting anything in return.

Scripture: "Each of you should use whatever gift you have received to serve others, as faithful stewards of God's grace in its various forms." - 1 Peter 4:10

Call to Action: Reflect on how serving others can open your heart to the Spirit's leading.

_____

_____

_____

_____

_____

_____

_____

_____

_____

_____

_____

_____

_____

_____

_____

_____

_____

Day 10: Express Creativity

Challenge: Engage in a creative activity that you enjoy, such as writing, painting, or playing music.

Scripture: "For we are God's handiwork, created in Christ Jesus to do good works, which God prepared in advance for us to do." - Ephesians 2:10

Call to Action: Consider how expressing your creativity can help you connect with the Spirit's inspiration.

_____

_____

_____

_____

_____

_____

_____

_____

_____

_____

_____

_____

_____

_____

_____

_____

Encouragement Midway Through

Dear Friend,

Congratulations on reaching the halfway point of the **20-Day Challenge: Intentionally Listening to the Spirit!**

I hope you've been enjoying this journey of spiritual discovery and growth. By now, you've likely experienced moments of deeper connection with the Holy Spirit, perhaps through quiet reflection, prayer, or acts of service.

It's natural to have days when you feel more connected to the Spirit than others. The key is to keep practicing, keep listening, and keep your heart open to the Spirit's guidance.

Remember, this challenge is not about achieving perfection. It's about cultivating a deeper relationship with the Holy Spirit and learning to rely on its presence in your life.

Keep going! You're doing great. I'm excited to see how the rest of this journey unfolds for you.

With encouragement,

Alisa L. Grace

Day 11: Spend Time in Nature

Challenge: Go for a walk in nature, paying attention to the beauty and wonder around you.

Scripture: "The heavens declare the glory of God; the skies proclaim the work of his hands." - Psalm 19:1

Call to Action: Reflect on how the natural world can reveal God's presence and the Spirit's work.

_____

_____

_____

_____

_____

_____

_____

_____

_____

_____

_____

_____

_____

_____

_____

_____

_____

_____

Day 12: Practice Forgiveness

Challenge: Forgive someone who has hurt you, releasing any resentment or bitterness.

Scripture: "Bear with each other and forgive one another if any of you has a grievance against someone. Forgive as the Lord forgave you." - Colossians 3:13

Call to Action: Consider how forgiveness can create space for the Holy Spirit to work in your life.

_____

_____

_____

_____

_____

_____

_____

_____

_____

_____

_____

_____

_____

_____

_____

_____

_____

Day 13: Read a Spiritual Book

Challenge: Read a chapter from a book that inspires your faith and encourages spiritual growth.

Scripture: "All Scripture is God-breathed and is useful for teaching, rebuking, correcting and training in righteousness." - 2 Timothy 3:16

Call to Action: Pay attention to any passages that resonate with you and seem to speak to your current situation.

_____

_____

_____

_____

_____

_____

_____

_____

_____

_____

_____

_____

_____

_____

_____

_____

_____

_____

_____

Day 14: Be Mindful of Your Words

Challenge: Choose your words carefully today, speaking with kindness and compassion.

Scripture: "Let your conversation be always full of grace, seasoned with salt, so that you may know how to answer everyone." - Colossians 4:6

Call to Action: Reflect on how your words can be a reflection of the Spirit's presence in your life.

_____
_____
_____
_____
_____
_____
_____
_____
_____
_____
_____
_____
_____
_____
_____
_____
_____
_____

Day 15: Practice Discernment

Challenge: When faced with a decision, take time to pray and seek the Spirit's guidance.

Scripture: "If any of you lacks wisdom, you should ask God, who gives generously to all without finding fault, and it will be given to you." - James 1:5

Call to Action: Trust that the Holy Spirit will lead you in the right direction.

_____

_____

_____

_____

_____

_____

_____

_____

_____

_____

_____

_____

_____

_____

_____

_____

_____

Day 16: Let Go of Control

Challenge: Surrender your worries and anxieties to God, trusting in His plan for your life.

Scripture: "Cast all your anxiety on him because he cares for you." - 1 Peter 5:7

Call to Action: Embrace the peace that comes from letting go and allowing the Spirit to lead.

_____

_____

_____

_____

_____

_____

_____

_____

_____

_____

_____

_____

_____

_____

_____

_____

_____

_____

Day 17: Be Open to New Experiences

Challenge: Step outside your comfort zone today and try something new.

Scripture: "For I know the plans I have for you," declares the Lord, "plans to prosper you and not to harm you, plans to give you hope and a future." - Jeremiah 29:11

Call to Action: Be open to the ways the Holy Spirit might be leading you in new directions.

Day 18: Share Your Faith

Challenge: Share your faith with someone today, either through your words or actions.

Scripture: "But you will receive power when the Holy Spirit comes on you; and you will be my witnesses in Jerusalem, and in all Judea and Samaria, and to the ends of the earth." - Acts 1:8

Call to Action: Trust that the Holy Spirit will give you the words to say.

_____
_____
_____
_____
_____
_____
_____
_____
_____
_____
_____
_____
_____
_____
_____
_____
_____
_____

Day 19: Reflect on Your Journey

Challenge: Take time to reflect on how your relationship with the Holy Spirit has grown over the past 19 days.

Scripture: "But grow in the grace and knowledge of our Lord and Savior Jesus Christ." - 2 Peter 3:18

Call to Action: Write down the ways you have become more attuned to the Spirit's voice.

_____

_____

_____

_____

_____

_____

_____

_____

_____

_____

_____

_____

_____

_____

_____

_____

_____

_____

Day 20: Continue Listening

Challenge: Commit to continuing to intentionally listen to the Holy Spirit in your daily life.

Scripture: "And I will ask the Father, and he will give you another advocate to help you and be with you forever— the Spirit of truth." - John 14:16-17

Call to Action: Reflect on the past 20 days. What practices have helped you connect with the Holy Spirit? How will you incorporate these practices into your daily routine moving forward? Write a prayer of commitment to continue seeking the Spirit's guidance.

_____

_____

_____

_____

_____

_____

_____

_____

_____

_____

_____

_____

_____

_____

Congratulations!

Dear Friend,

Congratulations! You've completed the **20-Day Challenge: Intentionally Listening to the Spirit!**

I'm so proud of your commitment to deepening your relationship with the Holy Spirit. Over the past 20 days, you've taken intentional steps to quiet your mind, open your heart, and listen for the Spirit's gentle guidance.

I hope this challenge has been a meaningful experience for you. Perhaps you've discovered new ways to connect with the Spirit, experienced greater peace and joy, or gained a deeper understanding of God's love for you.

Remember, this is just the beginning. Continue to cultivate your relationship with the Holy Spirit through prayer, reflection, and service. The Spirit is always with you, ready to guide and empower you on your journey of faith.

Well done!
With blessings,
Alisa L. Grace

Meet the Author

Alisa Ladawn Grace is an inspiring author, educator, and life coach passionate about guiding others toward spiritual growth, personal transformation, and meaningful relationships. With a Specialist Degree in Curriculum and Instruction and years of experience as a school administrator and nonprofit leader, Alisa combines her expertise in education with her deep faith to create impactful and relatable resources for readers of all ages.

In her latest book, *Powered* by the Spirit: Growing in Kindness and Forgiveness, Alisa invites readers to explore the life-changing role of the Holy Spirit. Through the relatable journeys of Ahlani, Nia, and Lenny, she demonstrates how the Holy Spirit can empower individuals to navigate challenges, build stronger friendships, and grow in kindness and forgiveness. With engaging stories, fun activities, and practical insights, this book is a guide to unlocking the incredible power of God's presence in everyday life.

Alisa's work extends beyond this title to include other transformative books, such as *Where Are the Fishers of Men? The Great Commission: Lost in the Crowd!* calls readers to embrace the mission of discipleship, and *No Turning Back: Breaking Free from the Grip of Yesterday* encourages readers to step into a life of freedom and purpose. In *Renewed: The Transformational Power of Putting Off the Old and Putting On the New*, Alisa explores the beauty of spiritual renewal and living in alignment with Christ's teachings.

Her writing is rooted in heartfelt storytelling, biblical truths, and practical personal and spiritual growth tools. Alisa believes that every individual has the potential to reflect Christ's love in extraordinary ways, and her mission is to help others discover that power within themselves.

Through her books, coaching, and leadership, Alisa Ladawn Grace inspires readers to embrace the guidance of the Holy Spirit, nurture meaningful relationships, and live lives filled with grace, compassion, and purpose. With her inspiring works, you can unlock your inner superpower and embark on a journey of growth!

www.ingramcontent.com/pod-product-compliance
Lightning Source LLC
LaVergne TN
LVHW051430080426
835508LV00022B/3334